Friday Reflections

Visit www.booksurge.com to order additional copies.

Friday Reflections

Anand Shah

2007

Friday Reflections

Contents

Acknowledgements

To friends and family around the world: Your feedback and encouragement on weekly Friday Reflections was the fuel that provided the motivation to publish this book. I am grateful to all of you.

Roger von Oech: Special thanks for taking me into the depth of creative spirit through your books: <u>Expect the Unexpected or You Won't Find It</u> and <u>A Whack on the Side of the Head.</u> I really appreciate your kindness in giving me permission to reprint your stories.

Billi Lim: My friend, thank you for inspiring me to "Dare to Try" and dare to tell your story in this book.

John Foppe: After listening to <u>One step at a time</u>, and reading your life story <u>What is your excuse?</u> I am learning to make the most of what I have. Thanks for allowing me to share our first encounter with the readers.

Warren Buffett: Your life is an inspiration. Thank you for allowing me to share your wisdom.

Don Yaeger: Thanks for allowing me to use quotes from <u>Never Die Easy</u>, a remarkable life story of my hero, Walter Payton.

Papa: Malav and I still remember our childhood days and wonderful stories that you told us during the evening rides. Every one of them had some key lesson.

Mama: Your second greatest gift to me was developing the life long love for reading.

My Lola: No life story has inspired me more than yours.

C P Low: You had the vision to develop Out of the Box Thinking class and courage to push it with passion.

S H Wong: Thanks for encouraging Out of the Box Thinking and giving me an opportunity to teach in Asia.

Gidu Shroff and Louis Liang: Your constant mentorship through the years is appreciated.

Walter Payton: You still live in the hearts you left behind.

Vajubhai: You taught us the real meaning of education.

Cynthia Kwon, Dave Hightower, Malav, Tejal, Mihir, Aarti, and The Chens (Dennis, Ping, Kevin, Oliver and Edwin): Thanks for your encouragement. Glad that we are one big family.

Analisa, Neil and Rajiv: Your enthusiasm, persistence and positive attitude are contagious. Thanks for your efforts in making this book a reality.

And

Luisa: My childhood penpal and our children's mother, whose everlasting support, encouragement and love has made life so meaningful.

This book is dedicated to

Perfect Souls: Those who teach the road to everlasting life in a liberated state.

Great Saints: Who have attained perfect knowledge and liberated their souls of all karma.

Great Masters: Who have gained mastery over a given subject.

Great Teachers: Who have properly interpreted the work of the above three and shared it with mankind.

And

Great People: That Dare to Dream, Dare to Try, Dare to Fail, Dare to Persevere and Dare to Win:

To all these great souls from whom I have acquired whatever little knowledge I have.

I bow down and dedicate this work.

Dedication is derived from The Universal Prayer (Navkar Maha Mantra)

Preface

Friday Reflections began when I was a little girl growing up in the heart of Silicon Valley. Every Friday, after dinner; my father, mother, brother and I would pile into our beat up, light yellow, 1983 Volvo to go for our weekly rides. During these rides, which would last about an hour, my father would regale us with all sorts of intriguing stories. Always, there was a little touch of humor, but there was also something a little more: a lesson to be learned. The stories were almost always from his childhood or his current life in the high tech world. My father told these stories in such a casual way that my brother and I never felt like we were in school being lectured; we just enjoyed listening to the stories.

These drives continued for years and years. No matter how long my father had worked through the week, he always had enough energy to take us out on those magical Friday night rides. My father is a great storyteller. Even to this day, he can tell a story with people so intrigued from beginning to end. We loved the stories and thought he was a fun dad.

Time passed till my brother and I reached our teenage years. The time we spent at home grew less; and the ability to get all four of us together on a Friday night, even any night, was nearly impossible. Eventually, my brother and I left for college and the stories stopped completely. We had started our own journeys out into the world.

One Friday night, before I headed out the door with some friends, I logged into my email account. An email awaited in my inbox. It read: *Friday Reflections.* It was from my father. I opened it up; and there was one of his stories told in an email, just as if I were a little girl again sitting in the backseat of a 1983 light yellow Volvo listening intently to her dad.

By 2004, *Friday Reflections* was being distributed to hundreds of friends over the World Wide Web. Now, in 2007, with insistence from many friends from all over the world to start a book of *Friday Reflections:* my brother Rajiv, our friend Neil, and I embarked on making these stories available to others. This book is the result of our efforts.

We only hope you enjoy reading these stories as much as my brother, I and many friends have through the years.

Analisa Shah

I.

If you don't have dreams how can they come true?

Once you have a dream, you need a set of values and disciplines working in harmony to make it come true.

Here are seven such values and disciplines:
1. **Keep on learning new skills:** They will never abandon you until your mind does.
2. **Assume Responsibility:** If you see an opportunity or a problem, you own it.
3. **People and Relationships:** It is people who make things happen, not machines.
4. **Flexibility:** "If you want to be successful in this fast moving world, be ready to change the document before the ink is dry." (Robert Noyce's advice to me in 1984.)
5. **Take Risks:** That is the only way to realize your true potential.
6. **Passion:** Do things with passion. It is contagious.
7. **Performance and Results:** In the final analysis, it is the value that you bring to the society.

And Always Remember:
Everything is OK in the end. If it is not OK then it is not the end.

The cover page represents the concept outlined in this reflection. Each one of the seven birds is carrying one of the above values while moving in the direction of their destination.

2.

What is the secret of successful people?

"The secret of success is constancy of purpose."
—Benjamin Disraeli

Story Line:

Many people have achieved their own success. A lot of people will look at them and wonder as to how they were able to achieve so much.

However, there are a few things that they all have in common.

1. They decide on exactly what it is that they love to do and they set goals. They have an extremely clear focus and see a path that can lead them to their destination.

2. Then, they make the necessary sacrifices to achieve it. They work extremely hard toward their goal knowing all the sweat will be worth it in the end.

3. And finally, they go after it with passion to become the best at it and never look back.

Reflection:

The beauty of this secret is that it is not exclusive to any race, culture, gender, national origin, industry group or educational level. All that it takes is three simple facts narrated above.

3.

"Do or Die" or "Do or Do"?

"The first rule is not to lose. The second rule is not to forget the first rule."

- Warren Buffett

Story Line:

"Do or do" is a famous quote from Mahatma Gandhi.

The expression most familiar with people is *"Do or Die."* However, when studying the lives of great achievers, it is very clear that losing was never an option when they pursued their dreams.

For the great achievers, it is *"Do or do."*

1. Ask any great basketball player before a game, "How many baskets do you plan to make today?" and the answer will be, "Every time I take a shot."

Ask any great baseball player about his day. And you will hear, "I plan to get a hit every time I step up to the plate."

From great baseball players you will never hear, "Well, if I get 2 hits out of five at bats, it would be a good day."

Great athletes do not give up their shots or 3 hits, even before the game begins.

This is also true for the winners in many other games of life. They expect to succeed in any task that they accept.

Such people strongly believe that if they expect anything less than the best, then they don't deserve to play the game.

2. For Gandhi, independence of India from British was the only option.

3. For Martin Luther King, "Free at last," was the only cause.

4. When Ali went into the boxing ring, the only plan he had was to come out as the winner.

5. Three young people I know started a business in their twenties. "'Come What May,' we are going to succeed" is their motto.

Reflection:

All achievers in life have a plan to win. Losing is never an option.

4.

Three mistakes a leader should avoid.

"The best executive is the one who has sense enough to pick good men to do the job, and self restraint to keep from meddling with them while they do it."

-Theodore Roosevelt

Story Line:

Wisdom of the ages: Ancient Chinese saying:

Three mistakes a leader or a manager should avoid:

1. Having good people and not know them

2. Knowing good people and not use them

3. Using good people and not trust them

Reflection:

This wisdom applies not only at work but in personal life as well.

The role of a leader or a parent is to instill good values in their employees and children, provide a healthy environment, and then trust that they will execute their tasks well.

5.

Getting a high return on your personal assets (From the life of Helen Keller)

Conquer the limitations you have set upon yourselves and you will discover a world of possibilities.

Story Line:

When I was in school, I had known about Helen Keller. At that time, the knowledge that she was deaf and blind, but still could do some things, was useful in answering the questions in quizzes or exams to get grades. The real impact of her remarkable life story had not sunk in until I read about her life during the 2004 Christmas holidays.

It is amazing how people like Helen Keller, with so many physical limitations, produced great things and delivered incredible return on limited personal assets — for themselves, and the world.

At the age of nineteen months Helen fell ill and became blind and deaf.

Reading further, I found it so amazing how she learned the meaning of words and then learned to write. She would smell or feel something and then ask her mentor to spell out the words in her hands. Over time, she learned four languages: English, German, French and Greek.

With her determination, hunger for knowledge and persistence, she became the first deaf and blind person to earn a Bachelor of Arts degree.

During her life, she wrote many books such as: <u>The Story of My Life</u>, <u>The World I Live In</u>, <u>Light in my Darkness</u>. In 1962, the movie, "The Miracle Worker," about Helen's life earned two Academy Awards.

Helen refused to dwell on her "handicaps." She lectured all over the world and promoted social and racial causes. In the process she raised money for blind people.

Reflection:

The story of Helen's life has provided inspiration to people around the world.

Beyond motivation, the lessons from her life are something worth pondering and worth exploring <u>before complaining about the lack of resources in your daily life.</u>

6.

Who is the most important salesperson of all?

Growth comes in seeing possibilities beyond the immediate circumstances.

Story Line:

The best salesperson I have known once told me, "In sales, getting inside the customer's door is half the job."

Businesses spend sizable amounts of money in marketing, advertising, promotion, events and travel, to get inside the customer's doors. Only after that, they can talk about the merits of their products or services, make a sale, and deliver performance that can eventually establish the brand image. (Good Will)

Now think about the situation where many potential customers are knocking on your door every day, without you having to spend the money. For a business, this sounds like a field of dreams. ("Wait, he is on to something.")

This happens when suppliers, job applicants and many other visitors come to your company's doors. Though they come knocking on your door for an opportunity to get your business or a job, you also have a golden opportunity to make a lasting impression about your brand. Negotiate hard, interview tough, but ultimately how you treat them as people and how you carry yourself as the representative of your company makes the difference in winning the hearts and minds of potential customers everyday.

Now a salesperson would say, "This is what dreams are made of. Is this heaven?"

In a nutshell;
Coffee and Donuts: $2.00
Common Courtesy: A smile and a warm handshake
Good will: Priceless
For Everything Else? (Nope, not what you expect)

It is: Yours and Your Company's Brand Image

Reflection:

1. Look at your job as much broader than as described in your job description.
2. Imagine: "I am the CEO of what I am responsible at work."
3. Anytime you are dealing with any person, it is your opportunity to build relationships and good will.
4. You are not only enhancing the brand image of your employer but you are also building or enhancing your own brand.

7.

Challenging the rules

"Every act of creation is first of all an act of destruction."
-Pablo Picasso

Story Line

Challenging the Rules: From <u>A Whack on the Side of the Head</u> by Roger von Oech.

If constructive patterns were all that were necessary for creative new ideas, we'd all be creative geniuses. Creative thinking is not only constructive, it's also destructive. Creative thinking involves playing with what you know, and may mean breaking out of one pattern in order to create a new one. A very effective creative thinking strategy is to play the revolutionary and challenge the rules.

Example: In the winter of 333 B.C., the Macedonian general Alexander and his army arrive in the Asian city of Gordium to take up winter quarters. While there, Alexander hears about the legend surrounding the town's famous knot, the "Gordian Knot." A prophecy states that whoever is able to untie this strangely complicated knot will become the king of Asia. The story intrigued Alexander, and he asked to be taken to the knot so that he could attempt to untie it. He studied it for a bit, but after some fruitless attempts to find the rope ends, he was stymied. "How can I unfasten this knot?" he asked himself. Then he got an idea: "I will make up my own knot-untying rules." He pulled out his sword and sliced the knot in half. Asia was fated to him.

Reflection:

Challenging the rules is a good creative thinking strategy, but that's not all. Not challenging the rules brings with it at least two potential dangers. The first is that you can get locked in on one approach, method or strategy without seeing that the other approaches may be more appropriate. As a result, you may tailor your problems to preconceptions that enable you to solve them that way.

A second reason the rules should be challenged is the following phenomenon. It runs as follows:

1. We make rules based on the reasons that they make a lot of sense.
2. We follow these rules.
3. Time passes and things change.
4. The original reasons for the generation of these rules may no longer exist, but because the rules are still in place, we continue to follow them.

8.

Things that matter most

Doing things right is always good, but what matters most is doing the right things right.

Story Line:

National News Release: One big university announced today that they had fired their football coach. The announcement said, "The coach had a win-loss record that was much better than previous three coaches and his players had higher academic achievements than previous teams. His players and assistants loved him and the coach was a great human being with a high level of integrity and work ethics."

Now one may wonder, "Then why did he get fired?"

The announcement continued, "He did many things right from Sunday to Friday, but failed to win **the Big Games*** on Saturdays."

Reflection:

1. Having high degree of ethics in any encounter is always important. Having said that:
2. The process is relevant as long as it produces the expected results for which one was hired.

3. In work situations, if the final report is: "A for effort, F for result," then one must reexamine the efforts.

*The games against their arch rival colleges are called, "The Big Games."

9.

In business (as in sports), it's not over till it's over.

A winner never quits...

Story Line:

Sports teaches many good lessons for daily life. Today's reflection is about two sports triumphs or tragedies, depending on which side you were on. It also teaches key lessons for personal and professional life as well as competitive businesses.

1993 Wimbledon Women's final: Defending champion Steffi Graff vs. Challenger Jana Novotna. After an intense battle in the first set and losing at 7-6, Jana took control and won the second set 6-1 and quickly built up the lead of 4-0, (40-Love) in the third and deciding set. She was five points away from a victory.

What happened next changed the course of the game. Jana double faulted on the next serve. Disturbed with her mistake, Jana lost concentration for the rest of the match. Steffi, sensing her opponent's vulnerability, took calculated chances with her shots and pressured Jana by coming to the net more often. Frustrated, Jana did not win a single game after her double fault and Steffi Graf won the final set 6-4, and the championship.

1974 USC vs. Notre Dame College Football: Notre Dame had dominated the first half and led 24-0 a few seconds before the first half. Notre Dame was to kick off following their last touch down. Legendary USC Coach John MacKay decided to do something different. He sent his tailback, Anthony Davis, to return the kick instead of his regular kick-off receiver. Notre Dame kicked the ball deep into the USC end zone. Anthony Davis caught the ball and ran 104 yards in to the Notre Dame end zone.

The teams went into half-time with Notre Dame up 24 to 7. But the momentum had already shifted. The final score after the second half: USC won 55-24.

Reflection:

In any competitive encounter, when you are ahead don't take your eye off the ball even for a moment. And when you are behind, do not give up. Just take a moment to think, capitalize if the opponent lets up, or try an approach that the opponent does not expect.

A winner never quits. This is also true for Jana and Notre Dame. They lost in one event, but since then, Jana has won Wimbledon and Notre Dame has won many championships.

10.

When one door closes, another opens

"When one door closes, another opens, but we often look so long and so regretfully upon the closed door that we do not see the one which has opened for us."

- Alexander Graham Bell

Story Line:

"THE STORY OF BILLI LIM"

Billi Lim is one of the greatest Out of the Box Thinkers that I have met. He was born into a poor family of 14. He survived childhood abuse, a diet consisting of leftover bones and meat for daily existence, and had setback after setback his entire life.

Billi's story is of a man who had every disadvantage set against him but he focused on what he wanted out of life. He went after it with such a ferocious determination that he succeeded against the odds. Along the way, there were many failures. Billi compiled the stories of his failures and the failures of other people into a book: <u>Dare to Fail</u>. It was on Malaysia's New Straits Times' No. 1 bestseller list. Now, Billi is a successful motivational speaker.

Reflection:

"Don't worry about your failures (disappointments). In fact, you should record and keep them. You will be surprised how much people are prepared to pay to listen to your failure stories when you succeed."

-*Billi Lim, Author of No. 1 Bestseller* Dare to Fail

II.

The Little Climber that Could

"Technique and ability alone do not get you to the top—it is the will power that is the most important. This will power you cannot buy with money or be given by others—it rises from your heart."

-Junko Tabei, First woman ever to climb Mount Everest

Story Line:

The story of Junko Tabei is one of ambition and persistence. She had a love for nature and there was something about mountains that was breathtaking to her. Her aspirations were to climb the highest mountains.

These were unconventional dreams for a woman to have. Especially one who stood at a mere 4 feet 9 inches. However, Tabei made up for her small size in determination.

Finally, in the spring of 1975, Tabei achieved her dreams by leading an all-Japanese female expedition up Mt. Everest. On the way up, they encountered obstacles typical of the mountains. The most extreme was an avalanche which injured the climbers, but not severe enough to go back.

On May 16, 1975, Junko Tabei became the first woman in the world to reach the summit of Mount Everest.

Incidentally Tabei wasn't satisfied with just Everest. She is also the first woman to successfully climb the summits of the highest peaks on all seven continents.

Reflection:

Like Junko, all winners in life set high expectations. But whenever they are met with difficulties, and there will always be difficulties, they do not lower their expectations. They figure out different approaches to reach their ultimate goal and they keep going in the direction of their dream until they achieve it.

12.

"But I am too old"...It is never too late to start something new

Age is an issue of mind over matter. If you don't mind, it does not matter.

-*Mark Twain*

Story Line:

Many times, we hear people say, "I wish I could do that but now I am too old." Here are the real life stories of some people that will inspire you to think otherwise.

Michelangelo, renaissance period Italian, creator of the statue of David, the painter of the world famous *Scenes of Genesis* and *The Last Judgment*, was 71 years-old when he designed the dome of St. Peter's Basilica.

Giuseppe Verdi, a great composer of romantic operas, created one of his greatest works, *Falstaff* in 1893 at the age of 80.

George Bernard Shaw, the famous English playwright, who won the Nobel Prize in literature and an Academy Award for adapted screenplay, "Pygmalion", completed his last work, "Buoyant Billions" in his 90s.

Jimmy Carter, a science graduate, a farm owner, who later became the 39th President of the United States, devoted his time after the Presidency to serve worthy causes around the world. In 2002, at the age of 78, he was awarded the Nobel Peace Prize. He is a prolific author; and 12 of his 20 books have been published after the age of 70. At 82, he is still serving people and writing books.

My maternal grandmother was 65 years old when my grandfather passed away. She went back to school and got her first Bachelor's degree. After that she tried for a Master's degree in English Literature and failed twice. As a young child my memory of her was that she used to study hard, often late nights, constantly worrying about grades; and on the two occasions when she flunked, she was in tears and needed a lot of consoling by family and friends.

She believed that to go after your dream and fail is never a failure, but to have a dream and not go after it is the ultimate failure.

Reflection:

People do not grow old by living a number of years. They grow old when they start regretting what they did not do instead of thinking about what they can still do.

13.

Think, Dream, Act and Achieve

"The greater danger for most of us is not that our expectations are too high and we miss it, but that they are too low and we hit it."

-Michelangelo

Story Line:

This incident happened in a medium size corporation in mid-1993. The company stock was floating in the 20s.

One day, a meeting between sales, marketing and planning-logistics groups was getting heated. Sales had brought a very aggressive revised forecast for product sales. The planning people were busy referring to their notebooks and telling sales folks that it was impossible to meet the new forecast. They were constrained by our company's supply line capabilities.

At the high point of that dialogue, the vice president of product division entered the room and inquired what was going on. Each side explained their sides of the story with ample passion and data.

What followed has stayed with me forever:

Mr. VP went to the white board and started mumbling while writing on the board, "If we make the upper end of the new sales forecast, the revenue will be x amount of $$$$$. With that kind of revenue growth rate sustained over next few periods, and based on our margin projections, the net profit will be $$$. For that kind of profit, our earnings per share will be $3.00. For the current Price/Earning ratio, which is 30 for our industry, the stock price would be $90." As he finished his calculations on the board, he turned to the amused audience and asked, "Who in this room believes that this can not be done?"

Planning and logistics people slowly closed their books and their leader told the audience, "This will require miracles but we will see what can be done and get back to you."

The bottom line is that they stretched their imagination and found the extra capacity in the global supply line. The company exceeded revenue forecasts and Wall Street rewarded it handsomely by exceeding $90 stock price in that period.

Reflection:

Set high expectations that people can relate with. Then they will go an extra mile and investigate ways to fulfill them.

14.

Know thy customer and environment

Develop innovative value based solutions. A solution means that it solves the real problem

Story Line:

During an excursion to Kuala Lumpur, we passed by a very impressive building, the KL Railway Station. The tour guide told us a story that sounded much too familiar.

When construction on the station was underway, the blueprint had to be sent to the head office in London for central planning approval. At the London headquarters, the blueprint was revised so that the roof at the KL Railway Station could comfortably accommodate two feet of snow.

The driver cracked, "A century has passed since then, and Malaysians are still waiting for the snow."

This story reminded me of the pitfalls of central planning narrated through the ages. Not being close to the actual users and creating inefficient applications.

Reflection:

Plan for snow in Malaysia?

Also, during one of my trips to Philippines during the years' end, it was refreshing to hear the song, "I am dreaming of a White Christmas." The next requested song was, "All of my life I have been waiting..."

15.

When an opportunity knocks, don't go to wash your face

Many a times, it is in the split second decisions that the fortunes are made or lost.

Story Line:

When I was young, not afraid to be curious and naïve about social status and etiquettes, I asked a question to my grandfather. "Why is it that all these supposed to be very smart (learned) people are not as rich as these other folks whom we call Banias (street merchants)?" His answer lay in an ancient Indian story.

There were two roommates. One of them was called Learned and the other one was called Merchant. Learned was supposed to be very educated because he had read almost every book in the world, carried credentials from many well known schools, and knew many things about processes and procedures.

In contrast, Merchant was considered from the lower class because he had not read many books, did not even know the names of most of the institutions that Learned had gone to, and was ignorant about most of the things about processes and procedures.

Early one morning, Laxmi, the Goddess of Wealth, came to the door of these roommates with the intention of blessing one with a great fortune. Learned was an early riser and opened the door. Seeing Goddess Laxmi eagerly waiting to bless someone, Learned told her, "Please wait, let me wash my face and brush my teeth before I take your blessings on my forehead." Learned was only following instructions as it pertained to the local code of conduct. Learned rushed into the bathroom to wash his face.

While this was going on, Merchant woke up and went to the door. Seeing Goddess Laxmi, eager to bless somebody, Merchant wasted no time in putting his head forward and asked for her blessings. He decided that he would have the rest of his life to wash his face and brush his teeth, but knew that he might never see Laxmi again.

When Learned returned from the bathroom, Laxmi was gone. Merchant was the one blessed with fortune and good luck.

"And that's why Bania's (Merchants) are richer than the Learned people," said my grandpa as he finished the story.

Reflection:

The difference between a successful person and an unsuccessful person, between a successful business and an unsuccessful business, is not in the lack of ideas or opportunities, but in the lack of timely action.

Recognize when an opportunity is knocking at your door and quickly act upon it.

16.

"I make the difference" Administrative Assistants Day

Remember the people who are instrumental in your and your organization's success. A sincere and timely appreciation goes a long way.

Story Line:

In the early 1990s, while looking for a source of supply for our new design, I visited a potential supplier in Mountain View, California.

As I entered the lobby and went to the receptionist to announce my arrival and to register for entry inside the building, something on her desk caught my eye. It was a plaque that stated, "I make the difference."

Soon after, when our host escorted us into the building, I noticed again that the secretary of a CEO also had the plaque on her desk stating, "I make the difference."

Somehow, I could not get those images out of my mind and spent the drive back thinking, "Do they really make the difference?"

Secretaries, receptionists and many other administrative employees are the first line of defense or offense, whichever way one wants to call it, when external people call or visit your company. In many cases, they create the first impression about your company, your organization and your team.

Second, administrative assistants keep office logistics in order and keep things organized. This allows other people to focus on their core jobs without interruptions.

I remembered what one great leader had told me in my early age, "They are the backbones of your organization. Having a good administrative assistant is having a big asset in your portfolio."

So never forget these people behind the scene. What they do makes the big difference.

Reflection:

In the first year in industry in 1983, during one emergency need, my boss asked me to hand carry a purchase order all the way through management ranks for signatures.

That was my first exposure to the hierarchy of organizations. My curious nature caught on to two interesting learnings through that expedition....

The higher up I went in the chain, I noticed that the offices looked very organized. Further research revealed that the higher-ups had very good administrative assistants and they relied, or in other words, depended, heavily on them to manage daily office logistics.

Yes, they do make the difference.

17.

Alexander the Great & the battle of Issus

"Read and Reread the deeds of The Great Commanders; it is the only way to learn the art of war."

- Napoleon

Story Line:

One sunny day, Alexander, the son of King Philip of Macedonia was watching his dad's soldiers trying to tame a black stallion with no success.

When Alexander offered to tame the horse, people laughed. But he being the King' son, was given a chance.

Now Alexander being very observant from childhood had noticed that the horse was getting wild whenever he saw his shadow.

Alexander turned the horse in the direction of the Sun so the horse could not see his shadow. The stallion calmed down and Alexander climbed on his back. Impressed, King Philip said, "Son, look for the kingdom worthy for yourself, for Macedonia is too small for your talents."

And thus began the story of one of the greatest commanders who, in the ten year span before the age of 30, had conquered the land from Greece to Northern India. I have been thoroughly fascinated by Sikandar (as we call him in India) since the fourth grade when I first heard stories of him.

The defining moment that transformed him from Alexander to Alexander the Great came in the battle of Issus (now in Turkey): Alexander was faced with unexpected news that his opponent, King Darius with an army of 200,000 (Almost 6 times larger than Alexander's 35,000 person army) was behind him instead of front as he had anticipated. Darius had cut off his lines of supply and communication.

Alexander decided to make the most of the changed situation. He decided to take Darius head on. Darius, based on his benchmarking information, decided to fight in wide open plain where he thought his bigger army would be an advantage. He put his strongest troops on the right side of the field and decided to overwhelm Alexander with numbers and break his line of defense.

Alexander was one commander who led from the frontline and fought side by side with his soldiers. They were well trained to cope with harsh environments and rapidly changing situations. They had graduated from the school of hard knocks, used unconventional weapons and had strong work ethics. Eventhough they were small in numbers, they were big in their will to win.

Since his troops were mentally and physically well

prepared, Alexander, with his supreme confidence, took a big risk and shifted some of his troops from right side of the field and attacked the left side of his opponent. Not prepared for this unexpected event, Darius' army lost control. The commanders got involved in finger pointing. Without the direction from the top, the soldiers on the strong right side got confused. Darius fled and Alexander won.

The battle of Issus changed the course of history.

Reflection:

"Read and Reread the deeds of The Great Commanders; it is the only way to learn the art of war."

The lessons from this story are equally applicable to business and personal life.

18.

Just One

Process is relevant as long as it produces tangible business results.

Story Line:

Years ago, there was an advertisement on television by an airline that went something like this:

The advertisement opened with a scene where there were many reservation agents on phones with potential customers. Most of the agents seemed to be in a hurry. As soon as they hung up one call, they would pick up the phone from the next caller. But only a few percentages of their calls were resulting in the sale of tickets.

There was one agent, Debbie, who took a phone call from a guy from an army base. There were many other army fellows lined up behind him. In those days, there were no toll free lines and everyone was expected to have enough change for a phone call. It seems that, either the fellows in the line did not have change or did not want to spend a dime. So as soon as one finished his reservation, instead of hanging up, he handed the phone to the next person in line and that continued.

Debbie patiently and courteously handled all of them, and through one call, made many reservations. (My guess is 50+)

At the end of the day, the supervisor was taking her rounds asking each agent, "How many phone calls did you handle today?" (She was tracking activities)...Of course, most of the answers were "Twenty, Thirty...etc."

Now the supervisor reached Debbie's desk, "Debbie, how many phone calls did you handle today?"

Replied Debbie, "Just One"

Reflection:

Most employees will respond to whatever indicators are set for measuring success. If the primary indicator for success is related to process activity, they will confine their actions within that narrow domain; and stay away from exploring different ways to do things. In the end, the great many possibilities for creating better bottom line results will be lost.

19.

Shouldn't every day be a Mother's Day?

Is there anything such as a "Non Working" Mother?

Story Line:

In United States and some European countries, the 2nd Sunday of May is celebrated as a Mother's day. Some other countries celebrate at different times of the year.

History is filled with many stories of Mothers' love and sacrifices. Here is a story of one such mother.

Marie Curie: "I have frequently been questioned, especially by women, of how I could reconcile family life with a scientific career. Well, it has not been easy."

Marie Curie was born in Poland. Her parents, who were teachers, instilled the value of lifelong learning in their children. At a young age she lost her mother and one sister. She saved money for higher education and later got accepted for higher studies in Sorbonne, a famous French University. She became the first woman to receive a doctorate degree in France.

Later, with her husband Pierre, she discovered two new radioactive materials and named them Polonium and Radium. Radium opened the door for nuclear physics and created many advances in medical technology which lead to the treatment of cancer. In 1903, they were awarded the Nobel Prize in Physics for their work. She became the first woman to win the Nobel Prize.

When her husband died in an unfortunate street accident, she took his place as a professor at the University of Paris. Marie raised a young daughter through some real challenging years.

In 1911, Marie was awarded the Nobel Prize in Chemistry, her second one. Later, her daughter Irene also won the Nobel Prize. The Curie family is the only family in the world to have won four Nobel Prizes.

Reflection:

From Marie Curie's teachings:

1. Nothing in life is to be feared, only to be understood.
2. I never see what has been done; I only see what needs to be done.
3. Life is not easy for any of us. But what of that? We must have perseverance and above all confidence in ourselves. We must believe that we are gifted for something and that this thing must be attained.

20.

Doing brain surgery for a headache when an aspirin would have sufficed

"Common sense is not so common."

-Voltaire

Story Line:

The Time: Late 80s.

The Place: A small company with unique chipset products.

On one Friday morning, while the director of operations (Bill) was chatting with his employee, the CEO walked into his office and said, "Bill, I am on the phone with a potential customer. He is not happy with the performance of his current supplier and has approached us. I need production volumes and availability for our new products." Bill assured the CEO that he had the information and he would bring it to him.

Now, Bill was a guy who was a great devotee of PCs and all the wonderful gadgets and tools that it was bringing to the world. He had discovered "Harvard Graphics," the presentation software, only a month before and had a non-stop fascination for that toy.

Bill picked up a sheet of paper off his desk, on which there was already all the information about product builds and availability that the CEO needed, and started entering the data in the "Harvard Graphics" software. (Bill was not happy that the original information was written in pencil with few mark-up notes)

A few minutes later, the CEO walked in to Bill's office, with the color of his face as red as a South American Monkey, and said, "Bill, the customer just hung up the phone. I lost the opportunity. No executive in the United States has to put up with the pain that I have with you." And the CEO left.

Fuming, Bill asked his employee to close the door. Bill told his employee, "The CEO is unreasonable, insensitive, and does not get it. All that I was trying to do was to give him the presentation style material since it is for the customer."

The employee being loyal to Bill; gathered all his courage and told him, "Boss, all that you needed to do was hand him the original sheet of paper on your desk when he walked in the first time."

Sequel:

Bill is retired and lives in the woods in Montana. The employee is still working in the semiconductor industry and is doing bigger and better things. The whereabouts of the CEO are unknown. He may have found serenity in the forests of the Amazon (after dealing with more Bills in his career).

21.

Time and Tide waits for no one

"There is a tide in the affairs of men which, taken at the flood, leads on to fortune; omitted, all the voyage of their life is bound in shallows and in miseries."

-William Shakespeare

Story Line:

In the early 80s, while visiting "The happiest place on earth," a.k.a. Disneyland, two fellows ended up in The Bear County.

There they saw a show where different, large, and overstuffed toy bears and animals were singing country music songs. Seeing children and adults alike enjoying the show, these fellows got to talking after the show.

"What if we made a talking toy bear in a size that children can handle?" They saw an opportunity to put a singing bear in every home.

Even though initial impression and many subsequent signs were pointing to an incredible opportunity, those fellows kept gathering more and more data to justify their case. I guess they wanted to do a thorough risk assessment and proper risk mitigation before the start.

Now, the only trouble with ideas is that others can get them too. And in many cases, they can be the same ideas as yours.

While those fellows were busy researching and talking, a company named Worlds of Wonder introduced Teddy Ruxpin™, a talking teddy bear who could tell stories and sing similar to the ones in Bear County.

Reflection:

Teddy Ruxpin™ was introduced in 1985 and became a great success in the market.

Many people get ideas, some have huge potential for success. But it is only those who act in a timely manner and do something about it (sell, license or make); that get the opportunity to enjoy the rewards.

*Teddy Ruxpin™ is a registered trademark of Alchemy II and is sold by Backpack Toys

22.

Who was this man?

"Always bear in mind that your own resolution to succeed is more important than any other one thing"

- Abraham Lincoln

Story Line:

As a young man, he worked on a farm to support his family while educating himself without any formal schooling.

He started his own business and in 1831, his business failed leaving his partners in debt. A loyal man, he worked the following seventeen years to pay off his debt.

In 1835, his fiancée died and he suffered a nervous breakdown in the following year.

In 1838, he was defeated for speaker and then lost the nominations for congress in 1843 and 1848.

He was rejected for the title of land officer in 1849.

He ran for senate in 1855, but once again he was defeated.

In 1856, he ran for vice president and was defeated once again.

Finally, in 1860 he ran for Presidency and was elected as the sixteenth President of the United States of America.

Abraham Lincoln, one of America's greatest Presidents, suffered many setbacks on his rise to the top.

Reflection:

The difference between a successful person and an unsuccessful one is that a successful person does not give up when met with disappointments and failures. It is not how many times you get knocked down, but how many times you get up and try again.

23.

Hire for attitude, train for skill

Skills can be learned through training, but it is your attitude that determines your commitment to excellence.

Story Line:

Southwest Airlines is known for cheap airfares as well as excellent customer service. I have to agree, as I have flown with Southwest numerous times and any problem I have encountered has been settled pleasantly by Southwest personnel.

Southwest enjoys the record of having the fewest customer complaints of any company, and has received award after award for being able to retain customers. It is no surprise that, for thirty-two years, they have been consistently profitable.

So what exactly has Southwest Airlines figured out that makes them so successful?

Southwest believes that it is the people of Southwest, not the planes, that represents the company. Consequently, the company goes out of its way to hire the right employees who fit the company culture and provides a suitable environment for them to succeed.

"Hire for Attitude, train for skill" is what Southwest believes in. According to Southwest CEO Herb Kelleher, "You can train people for skills but you cannot train them for attitude." If a person does not have the right attitude, he does not belong in the Southwest team.

Many years ago, while looking for a person to manage our business systems, we interviewed a young man from Scotland who had just graduated with a Bachelor's degree in business. Knowing fully well that he did not have a degree in Information Systems or Computer Science (as was normally required for those kinds of jobs), we took into account the fact that he was a computer fanatic from the age of eight and displayed tremendous enthusiasm to tackle new challenges. It was a major risk taking, but the interview team felt that it was worth it.

The young man did not disappoint us. In five years that he spent with us, he delivered more solutions than his contemporaries and left positive impact on the operation as well as the majority of the people he touched.

So what was so special about this young man?

During the first month, he noticed that our small size group needed some key computer applications but was not receiving enough attention from central corporate group. He decided to learn programming himself. Instead of going to a full semester course with a fee of $3,600 that others had done, he bought a book for $32 and learned in a few weeks.

At work, he patiently listened to various internal customer groups' needs and then focused on delivering solutions rather than just system and tools. This was a refreshing change for customers since many internal groups were measuring their success by number of tools delivered instead of tracking if it had solved the customer's real needs.

Reflection:

With his "can do" attitude, focus on solutions, tremendous customer orientation, ability to get along with people and unlimited enthusiasm, he became a role model for many employees, junior and senior alike. We were richly rewarded for drafting a great attitude.

When he left to pursue his own venture, the stamp on his exit paper read "Eligible for Re-hire" as soon as he is available.

24.

Lessons of a Lifetime

"When I was a boy of fourteen, my father was so ignorant that I could hardly stand him around. When I turned twenty one, I was amazed how much the old man had learned in seven years."
- Mark Twain

Story Line:

Lessons of a lifetime learned by six friends between 1964 to 1969, from one great person: my father.

1. The most important relations are personal ones. Use the power of your finger to keep in touch on a daily basis. It is people who make things happen, not the machines.

2. In the future, women will be very dominant in all segments of world affairs. They are learning all the hard skills that men have and they have the soft skills that will be crucial for success in the new world.

3. No one gets poor by cashing in their profits. "Bulls will win, bears will win, but it is hoggers who will get slaughtered." Never buy on margin. Never play naked calls.

4. In sales, the important thing is not what you want to sell but it is what the other person wants to buy.

5. People with hands-on skills will never go hungry.

6. Never get in the middle of elephants' (people with power) fights, because there is an old African saying, "When the elephants fight, it is the grass (a small guy) that gets crushed."

7. Anyone who comes to your door should not leave empty handed. Treat them with respect, serve them a cup of tea; and when they depart, let them carry a lifetime of good will.

8. The world is too big. There are an abundance of opportunities. If you believe in yourself, there is always a room at the top for your talents somewhere in this world.

9. Relationships of the mind are temporary but the relationships of heart will stay forever.

10. Ask one more question. Try one more time.

His favorite quote was from Douglas MacArthur:
"An old soldier never dies. He only fades away."

25.

You can not win today's game on yesterday's press clippings

"We are what we repeatedly do. Excellence, then, is not an act, but a habit."

-Aristotle

Story Line:

A few years ago, a fellow approached a good friend to take advice about his work situation. Noticing that his job performance was declining, his supervisor had a friendly talk with him.

Now this fellow was very bright, carried credentials from well-known institutions and he had been a strong contributor and a star performer in the past. He was not pleased with his supervisor's feedback and needed some advice.

He told his good friend about many awards that he had received in years past, his numerous publications in journals, and speeches he had given at various conferences. He went on to emphasize that only a day before, he had seen a foil in someone's presentation that referenced the great work he did in the year 1999.

His good friend told him, "You already got paid for what you did in the year 1999. We are now in 2004, the next millennium. What have you done for your business lately?"

Good friend continued, "What you did yesterday is history. What you promise for tomorrow is mystery. What you can deliver today is reality. You can not win today's game on yesterday's press clippings."

The fellow became silent. He got the message. After that talk, his performance improved significantly.

Reflection:

We are in a dynamic and competitive world. Things are changing at such a rapid pace that the moment you let up, you fall behind. In today's world there are many people with drive, ambition and the right skills who are waiting for an opportunity. If you do not seize the opportunity, somebody else will.

Some people feel that they have "Paid Their Dues" with past success and the others owe them something in return. In reality, no one owes anything to us. Only we owe it to ourselves to plan on growing and succeeding.

Never rest on your laurels. Keep challenging yourself. Keep raising the bar and reach new heights.

26.

It's a wonderful life

"It is one of the most beautiful compensations of this life that no man can sincerely try to help another without also helping himself."

- Ralph Waldo Emerson

Story Line:

My mind keeps returning to the film, "It's a Wonderful Life." The film's message has stayed with me as it has with so many viewers. The message I took away was this: the truth of one's own life isn't in the taking, in the acquisition of more and more things, but of the giving of oneself to others. And that giving will impact those around you.

The central character, George Bailey, is not acting like his usual self in the beginning of the film. The townspeople pray to God for George. God responds by sending an angel to show Bailey the positive impact his life has made on his community.

Without going into a full-blown synopsis of the movie, I want to pose a few thoughts: Firstly, Bailey had always wanted to travel the world, and to leave the town that he was so integral to. Secondly, Bailey regretted the things he didn't do but never saw the positive influence he had in those around him. Why is it that the "what ifs" seem to occupy us more than the "what is?"

Finally, the angel showed George the purpose of his life and the good that was in his life all along.

Reflection:

The secret Bailey discovered was that you get what you give. If he had never given of himself to the community, the community would have suffered and George would have never affected the lives of so many people. The material things Bailey didn't acquire were replaced by the wishes, love, and thoughts of those he impacted in Bedford Falls.

As Bailey says at the end of the film, "No man can be poor as long as he has friends."

27.

Humor in the workplace

There is no better place than the workplace to find humor and relieve stress. All that you have to do is look, listen and learn to laugh.

Story Line:

True Stories from workplaces

1. More Data Needed?

    A meeting is going on between employees of a semiconductor supplier to review one customer's requirements. The customer is asking for an aggressive one-day response on Failure Analysis (FA) of the returned samples.

    The director of FA presents his current FA response time, which is 76 days. Another director raises his hand and asks, "Does your data include the weekends?"

2. A header note on a Fax: "Let me know if you do not receive this Fax."

3. While traveling in a foreign country superhighway, a visitor asked a toll collector, "I want to go to so and so beach. Which exit do I take?"

    Toll Collector: "Sir, take the second (exit) from the last."

4. A letter from a supplier to a customer explaining the reason for failing to deliver products on schedule.

    Dear Mr....We apologize...The delay in delivery was due to the issues related to our recent migration to an advanced planning and scheduling system called PROMIS.

5. A wall poster in a rest room in a foreign country: 2005: Please don't throw Butts in to Urinals. (I guess it meant Cigarette Butts.)

6. A wall poster in a company restroom in California in the early 90s:

```
DUE TO NEW WATER RATIONING
    EQUIPMENT INSTALLED...

IT IS NECESSARY TO HOLD THE
HANDLE DOWN A FEW SECONDS
LONGER THAN BEFORE WHEN
         FLUSHING

PLEASE BE SURE TO FLUSH THE
TOILET COMPLETELY.
```

28.

To a hungry man, give a piece of bread

To a hungry man give a piece of bread, and not thirty-two flavors, else he will throw up.

Story Line:

Many companies have training and development programs for their employees. In some places they are crisp and targeted to specific needs, while in other places they are extensive. Some of these extensive programs consist of exposing new hires to many different types of training classes in a short time while the others require employees to go through some massive training blasts that somebody has determined to be essential for revitalizing the company or whatever.

Whenever I am exposed to massive training blasts, I remember an incident from several years ago when I volunteered to take care of five kids during my sabbatical.

Trying to keep track of five kids and their activities was a massive planning and scheduling nightmare. I would pick up kids from different schools between 2PM to 3PM. Then the sequence was something like this: if it was 3PM then it must be swimming for Charlie; 3:30 was ballet for Gitanjali; but what about dropping Bobby to baseball at 4:15 while our kids were waiting after their swimming lessons?

Not to forget that Charlie went to karate after swimming and Gitanjali went to piano after ballet while Bobby had special math tutoring and our children needed to go to music classes. Well, the sequence did not end there but you get the idea.

One day, as my luck would have it, I got some time to ask questions to the kids.

I asked Charlie, "What did you learn today?"

"I don't know," came the reply from Charlie.

"And what about you, Gitanjali, what did you enjoy about the piano class?"

"You know, during the break we ran around sprinklers and got wet. That was fun," said Gitanjali with a visible excitement on her face.

Being aware of the conflict of interest situation, I did not dare to ask any specific question to our children. They would have taken the fifth any way.

My curiosity prevailed further and I asked a general question, "Why do you go to these classes?"

Came the unanimous reply, "Because our parents want us to."

I followed up with a question, "And what do you do with what you are taught in the classes?"

"When is the time to do something with what we are taught?" said our boy mustering up all his courage.

Reflection:

Further investigation and introspection revealed that these children were occupied in so many activities during the day that they had no time to practice and perfect any of them well enough.

This is what happens with giving an overdose of training to the new hires and delivering massive training blasts to all employees. The office shelves get full with training binders, checklist for "training completed" are in compliance, but what was taught is not put in to practice in most cases.

The cases where training has been highly effective is when it was targeted for specific needs, people were given enough time to absorb what was taught, and there was a follow up as to how training was put into practice.

29.

Breaking a Rookie into the game

In business or in sports, people are hired based on their good skills. The day of reckoning for a Rookie is when he/she is asked to perform in stressful situations like when the game is on the line and thousands of people are screaming.

Story Line:

Most organizations: corporations, sports teams, or studios, normally go through a rigorous screening process to select the right candidate for a job.

But what determines the success of the employee and/ or the team going forward? It not only depends on the talent (technical, hard-core skills) but also on the mental toughness (emotional, soft skills).

There is a dual responsibility here: on the employee, and a much more on the manager. Assessing when to break a person in different situations is an extremely important aspect of managing and coaching.

In the early 90s, a baseball team needed to win the final game of the season to get into the play-offs.

For the most crucial game of the season, the manager had two reliable veterans available to pitch but decided to go with a very promising, hard throwing rookie pitcher.

The manager possibly envisioned headline stories written about the boldness and "genius" of him and the guts of rookie if the gamble worked. But the fans who had watched the rookie's performances during the regular season were concerned that even though he was impressive and talented, he had not been tested in any high-pressure situations.

For those who watched the game, the rest is history. The opponent piled up a huge lead against the rookie pitcher by the third inning and the team never recovered. The most promising rookie of the year could not recover from the emotional shock and left baseball.

He returned to baseball a few years ago but has never been the same pitcher that his potential showed in early 90s.

With his decision on that fateful day, the manager did not do the right service for the team or for the career of a very promising young man.

Reflection:

This is an important lesson for managers and leaders in any field.

Before promoting a person or assigning him/her to manage crucial tasks in a high-pressure environment, assess if the person is psychologically prepared to handle that level of challenge. If not, give some more time in the coaching and preparation.

30.

"Bigger Station, Bigger Income"

For what does it benefit man if his status is raised when he himself is not raised?"
- Louis Fisher on Mahatma Gandhi's philosophy

Story Line:

When reading about scandals in politics and corporations, I often think about a movie, Bhuvan Shom, which won high marks in many International Film Festivals in 1969.

My recollection of the key events is as follows:

Bhuvan Shom is the railway stationmaster of a small train station in an even smaller town in India.

Bhuvan Shom has poor work ethics. He is known for taking bribes, being rude to customers, and frequently skipping work since there is no local supervisor to watch over him.

One day, the head of Indian Railways goes to that town for a vacation. For the first time, Bhuvan Shom shows up to work early and leaves late. He starts treating passengers with courtesy and stops taking bribes as a side business.

During his time in the town, the boss develops sympathy for Bhuvan Shom's poor family and decides to help him. The boss offers Bhuvan Shom a promotion and a higher paying job at a larger station in an equally larger town.

Just before his departure from the town, the boss gives him a tutorial on the code of conduct and emphasizes the need for high ethics.

As the boss is boarding the train, Bhuvan Shom assures him that he will be the role model for ethics.

As the train pulls out of the station and is out of sight, Bhuvan Shom exclaims, "Bigger Station, Bigger Income" (he meant an opportunity for bigger bribes).

Reflection:

The real change in the status of a person does not come from the change in position power or promotion, but through the transformation of character and values.

31.

When a meeting becomes a wrestling event

Meetings... What would we do if there were no meetings?

Story Line:

A long time ago, a father got dragged into watching a wrestling event by two young kids who were thoroughly fascinated by what they had heard from schoolmates about that kind of wrestling. The auditorium was jam-packed and Dad's initial impression was that this must be something really good to have attracted so many people.

The wrestlers had interesting names such as Millionaire, Money Machine, Megalomaniac, Know It All etc. As the event progressed, the crowd kept cheering their favorite wrestler whenever he knocked the other guy down, climbed up on the top rope and jumped on the fallen comrade. Every time that happened, there would be an explosion of cheers and the fallen fellow would seem to be in extreme pain. Eventually the referee would declare the winner, and amazingly, even the injured wrestler was able to get up and walk back to his dressing room. Dad was pretty convinced that the whole event was fixed.

On the way back home, one of the kids asked, "Dad, have you seen anything like this before?"

Replied the Dad, "Yep, I see this everyday at work."

"Wow! How come?" asked the excited kid.

"Well Son, We have many meetings at work that are just like what I saw today. You pretty much know the outcome before the event (meeting) begins but people still go through the motions (just like those wrestlers) and look seriously engaged. And there are certain seasons when more people get engaged and with a lot more intensity."

"And you get paid for all this fun?" exclaimed the other excited kid.

"Now wait a minute, this is not all that we do at work and this does not happen all the time either," cautioned the Dad, to ensure that the kids do not develop the wrong value system.

"Dad, do you have a Millionaire?"
"Yes, plenty," Dad replied.
"How about Money Machine?"........
"We call them Finance."
"And what about Megalomaniac and Know It All?"
"No Comment."

As they reached home, the kids went running to their mom and told her that the dad had a real fun job and that is the reason why he is spending a lot of time at work.

Reflection:

A meeting is a means to get valuable work done. If the meeting is going nowhere, do not go through the motions to fill time. Blow the whistle and stop it.

32.

"But it is the supervisors..."

"Everyone thinks of changing the world, but no one thinks of changing himself."

- Leo Tolstoy

Story Line:

Once upon a time, while teaching classes about creativity and risk taking, the teachers noticed an interesting phenomenon: The overwhelming feedback from the students from every class was, "Excellent class, but have our supervisors take this class." The underlying implication was that their supervisors were being roadblocks to acceptance of their creative ideas.

Further investigation revealed that in many cases, their supervisors and their supervisor's managers also had attended the class and they had said the same thing, which was, "Have our supervisors take the class."

It seemed that everyone believed that a change was needed, but they wanted someone else to change before they could do something about it.

Then I thought about the history of Silicon Valley, and also about the pioneers around the world. I thought about the eight people (Seagulls) from Shockley Semiconductor.

When their innovative ideas were not supported by their brilliant but autocratic boss, they dared to fly out of their flock to form Fairchild Semiconductor. They were called "Traitorous Eight" by their boss.

Fairchild began a new industry and put Silicon Valley on the world map. The process did not stop there. Many Fairchild Seagulls continued their exploration and contribution to the world by taking further risks and started many other companies and industries. In the course of their risk taking, they created products that have made a positive impact on the lives of millions of people around the world.

Reflection:

History is filled with the stories of such people all around the world. They have lived up to Mahatma Gandhi's motto, "I must be the change I want to see in this world."

Don't be encumbered by history, challenge the status-quo, dare to take risks, innovate and contribute positively to your community and our world.

You may find out that even your old supervisors are proudly telling others, "You know, he/she worked for me once upon a time."

33.

Reach Out and Thank Someone

"It is people who make things happen, not machines."
- Advice from one great person in 1965.

Story Line:

In the USA, the first Monday of every September is "Labor Day." Of course, it is a joyous time for people because it is an extra day off from work. But thinking differently, in terms of the original intent of Labor Day, it is the day to pay tribute to working men and women who contributed to the success of our country. Many other countries also have a similar day in different times of the year.

Even though I know the science behind how planes fly, I am always fascinated by how such a huge mass of body lifts and soars at 35,000 feet and safely takes people to distant shores in a few hours. So upon reaching my destination, whenever I get a chance to see the pilots while disembarking, I take an opportunity to thank them.

So during one such encounter when I thanked the pilot and told him, "I am amazed at how you get this massive machine to fly."
He replied, "So am I." The next sentence he uttered was very profound *"You know, it takes a lot to get it up there. There are a lot of people behind it."*

Reflection:

Isn't the same true for organizations, leaders and individuals? There are a lot of men and women behind what we accomplish. Even if we may have previously expressed our appreciation for their contributions, Labor Day is one more opportunity to reach out and thank people who have contributed to our success in many different ways.

34.

Parrot, Parrot who needs a Parrot?

More or less; what is better, "more with more or more with less?

Story Line:

A long time ago, there was an annual planning meeting taking place in a division of a rather large corporation. Different department heads presented the following year's plans and resources requirements.

Intense dialogues took place about the benefits of the projects and claims for more resources.

Just after a mid-afternoon break, the boss returned with a green parrot. Everyone in the room was amused. But then they had known their boss to be out of the box on so many occasions in the past that they assumed, "This must be one of those days."

Finally, the boss broke the silence.

He said, "Let me introduce you to Greg, the newest member of my staff." He pointed at the parrot. "Going forward he is going to be my vice president of sales, operations, engineering, etc."

People burst in to laughter thinking that the boss was in his "Expect the Unexpected" mood.

The boss continued, "And Greg is well trained. Every time I ask him to do new things he automatically replies, 'I need more resources.' And every time I say, 'You can't have more resources,' he replies, 'Then, I can not do so and so projects.'"

The boss went on and emphasized that since they should be cost conscious any time and not just some of the time, he had bought only a $300 Green Parrot instead of an expensive Macau to do the job. He was pretty sure that the extra elegance offered by Macau was of no further value.

Reflection:

The last thing the boss said, "Having said all this, I want to know from you, ladies and gentlemen, What else can you do for me that Greg can not?"

People are hired to think and find ways to accomplish things in better, faster and cheaper ways. Faced with new challenges, if all that they can think of is well known standard answers then why would an employer need them?

35.

In Asia, most of the business is done over a cup of tea

The most important relations are personal ones

Story Line:

In 1980, when I graduated from college, the company that I was working for offered me an expatriate job in Manila, Philippines. I would be working for a senior expatriate who was already stationed at a subcontractor plant. The opportunity to work in a foreign country seemed exciting, and I gladly accepted.

Just before I left, I paid a courtesy visit to Mr. David, the general manager of our division. I asked him if he had any words of wisdom about how to thrive in a foreign country.

He told me, "Young man, in Asia most of the business is done over a cup of tea." Then he shook my hands and wished me well.

Hmm!! That seemed very profound advice. I spent most of the plane ride trying to debug what he really meant. I even wondered, "If all that it took is a cup of tea to do business in Asia then why did I spend all these years sweating over a degree?" Young that I was, I did not grasp the key concept behind Mr. David's statement.

In the first few days I noticed that, every morning, my boss and the other expatriates spent time with Mr. Chang, proud owner of the very first subcontractor assembly facility in Asia, talking about all kinds of world affairs over their morning coffee or tea. I observed that they were not talking about 'Real Business', our company's business, and I felt uncomfortable about it.

So in the next week, when I requested a meeting with Mr. Chang to go over my agenda and instead I got an invitation to join him for a cup of tea, I refused. I wanted a formal meeting.

I got a call back from his secretary that for the next three weeks, Mr. Chang was busy with bankers, labor union and a visit to the Presidential palace. For a formal meeting, I would have to wait.

Three weeks? That was an eternity for one who comes from a competitive environment and wants to prove his worth to the company right away. I went and complained to my local boss and asked him what to do. Amazingly, his advice was, "Go and have a cup of tea."

I thought, "What is wrong with all these people?"

Anyway, I realized that it was the best option under the circumstances. So the next day I went for a cup of tea. The same thing happened in the following two days, a tea and world affairs. By Friday, I was getting impatient. To my surprise, Mr. Chang inquired about my plans. In a few minutes after I started describing the details, he summoned three key managers to his office and told them, "Give Mr.

Shah whatever support he needs." Unconditional support? Wow! No negotiations. I had cut a good deal without much effort.

What followed was a great teamwork with his people and a huge improvement in yields and quality. The word of our accomplishments traveled across the oceans. It was evident on Mr. David's face when he came for his annual visit to Asia.

Sequel to the Story:

Not long after that, we received a surprise shipment at our home. The sender was a US branch of our company. It contained appliances that my wife and I needed, but could not afford. Those appliances were of a famous brand, made by a subsidiary of our parent company.

Nervous, I called our secretary to ask if she knew anything about it since I did not order them and I did not have the savings to pay for them.

She informed me that they were from Mr. David and there was a telex from him: "In Asia, most of the business is done over a cup of tea. Thanks, for your hard work and great results."

Note: This story narrates my experience in Asia. However, similar practices do exist in other parts of the world over a glass of beer or over a golf game or while enjoying a hukka.

36.

Are you busy? Humor in High Places

If so many people were not so busy describing how busy they are, they wouldn't be that busy after all

Story Line:

One of the most fascinating things in this fast moving world is that not a day goes by without some humor in it.

You are busy working on a computer with your back facing your office entrance and your mind is deeply engrossed in solving a problem. Suddenly, you hear a knock on the door.

You turn around. The person at the door asks in one breath, "Are you busy? Do you have a minute?"

Your answer at this crucial moment, inflexion point as some would call it, shapes your destiny for the time that follows.

You almost want to say, "What do you think?" Or possibly, "No, no, I was just waiting for you to drop by and bless my office with your kind presence."

But you really think that it will actually only be a minute as proclaimed, your sense of duty towards a fellow worker prevailing, and you say, "Come on in. How are you doing?"

And the visitor obliges you with, "I am very busy and behind on commitments. I don't have enough time in the day to finish it all....Our company needs to do a better job with work-life balance."

Reflection:

And soon after that half an hour-long (supposed "one minute") discussion, both of you fall behind on your tasks and stay late to catch up on your commitments. Such is the irony of fate when you don't manage your time effectively.

37.

Life is a self-fulfilling prophecy. You Get What You Expect

"Treat a man as he is and he will remain as he is. Treat a man as he can and should be and he will become as he can and should be."

- Goethe

Story Line:

Several years ago an experiment was done in a school where, in the beginning of a school year, incoming students were classified in two groups; those who will do very well, and those who will be lower performers. This was not based on any data related to past records or their abilities, but just done arbitrarily. This information was then shared with teachers and students. Lo and Behold, the end of the year performance correlated well with the initial classification. The teachers treated students based on the information provided to them and students performed consistently with the initial expectations and ratings, no matter their real capabilities.

Author Roger von Oech describes this phenomenon as the self-fulfilling prophecy, where a person believes something to be true which may or may not be so, acts on that belief, and by his actions causes the belief to become true. The self-fulfilling prophecy is a case where the world of thought overlaps with the world of action. And it happens in all avenues of life.

Similarly for organizations, if employees believe that their organization will be the best it can be, they will do everything possible to make it as such. If employees believe that high growth rate and great stock price are achievable, they will stretch their imagination to reach those targets. And through this process, they will propose fundamental changes, bring many innovations and find creative ways to add real value in their products. Once stockholders believe in the authenticity of their actions, the self-fulfilling prophecy kicks in.

Similarly, leaders who believe in their people and expect the best from their teams will get the best.

Reflection:

From the book, <u>A Whack on the Side of the Head</u> by Roger von Oech

"What about us, the individuals? When you look in the mirror in the morning, see the face of the person who is going to accomplish wonderful things in personal and professional life. Life is a self-fulfilling prophecy. You get what you expect."

38.

The Road Less Traveled

"Two roads diverged in the wood
And I took the one less traveled by
And that has made all the difference"
                    - From a Poem by Robert Frost

Story Line:

Prior to Christopher Columbus' voyage to America in 1492, the known path to India was going east via the African coastline.

Christopher Columbus decided to travel westward to reach India. The scientists, navigators and experienced travelers of the time thought that he was crazy.

So when Columbus approached King of Portugal for venture money to sponsor a voyage to India via the western route, he received a "No, Thank You." The King had already invested in plans to reach India through the eastern route.

Columbus received similar responses from crowns in Spain, France and England. But he did not give up — I guess some people never learn from existing data. Finally, Queen Isabella and King Ferdinand of Spain did put seed money in to Columbus' venture. The rest is history.

Reflection:

The key difference between Columbus' voyage and other contemporary explorers of his time was that Columbus took the road less traveled. And in the process he discovered a new continent and unlimited opportunities for the people who followed.

39.

"Bust the Bureaucracy"

"There was a boy who killed both his parents; and during the court proceedings, pleaded mercy on the ground that he was an orphan."

—From an Abraham Lincoln Story

"If people do not have discipline to know the value of and use what they already have, what makes you think they will have discipline to carry through on new programs?"

Story Line:

A few decades ago, the CEO of a corporation was faced with a dilemma. The revenue growth was slowing down from the fast pace of previous years and the competition was intense.

Customer complaints about the quality of service were on a rise. He had also noticed that it was getting difficult to get things done in a timely manner inside the company.

So, per the advice of some close associates, he hired an external consulting firm to assess the situation. The external firm immediately went to work. They studied the situation in detail and reported the findings.

The report started with a punch line, "There is massive confusion amongst employees between things that need to happen vs. things that do not need to happen."

After many pages of information in the middle, the report concluded, "The company's operations have become very bureaucratic. This is not sustainable in the current market environment. The company needs immediate attention and a major overhaul."

Being alarmed, the CEO immediately launched a company-wide campaign. It was named "Bust the Bureaucracy." He wanted "All Hands" to join forces in cleaning up the non-productive processes, methods and systems. "Scrutinize everything, don't assume anything" was the directive.

To accomplish this massive task, a corporate level "Bust the Bureaucracy" task force was formed. This task force defined the overall structure for the campaign, top level champions, process and sub-processes team leaders and the team members. Suggestion boxes and "town meetings" were introduced for common, working level employees to have their say.

Now, some employees were intrigued that some of the higher ups (very high up) whose departments had a lot of bureaucracy had become the champions for this new task force. It looked as if the masters who had created bureaucracy had now become the champions of busting it.

But for those who had been around for a while, and understood the games that are played in such type of organizations, knew that "The Masters" had no choice but to become "The Champions." That was the only way for them to control the work and pace of the various teams and also manage what was going to be reported to the CEO.

Before I get back to the CEO, let us also visit one of the sub-campaigns that started as a result of this program. Based on the employee feedback, the Champions had identified, "Are we having too many meetings?" as one of the ingredients to Bust the massive Bureaucracy.

So the General Manager of division in the North part of the state specially called for some additional consultants that he knew in the South to address the "Meetings" issue.

Immediately upon arrival, the husband/wife consultants tag team began their work. They set up three meetings with each employee; the first one for introductions, the second one for details, and the third one for conclusions. On top of that they also set up group meetings to tap the combined power of masses. Employees noticed that in each of those meetings, the husband asked questions and the wife made notes.

Finally arrived the day of reckoning. The CEO had decided to travel to every shore and touch every division to listen first hand to his "Champions" revelations; followed by the famous last words, "What are we going to do about it?"

The celebration, in other words "to ease the pain" session, was set up one Thursday in an external lodge with a nice dinner, to be followed by the General Manager's presentation (Or confessions, as some employees humorously called it).

There is an old saying, "After feast comes the reckoning," and it was no different that night. The General Manager got up and "honestly/candidly" shared the task force findings.

To sum it up:
1. The division had lost focus on what the real customer wanted.
2. There were too many processes and systems that were set up with good intention of servicing internal needs, but instead they were hampering employees from doing their jobs. (Example: Changes required up to 69 approvals)
3. The people were very busy and stressed with numerous activities, but the output could not be linked to any bottom-line business indicators.

Some employees, while listening to the speech, even wondered why the GM was not taking protection under the Fifth Amendment. Of course, the candid GM also presented "Get Well Plan" and organization to address it.

Sequel to the Story: following Monday, employees were summoned to mandatory "All Hands Meeting." They were shocked to see CEO again, so soon, at their site.

The CEO started "I will be very brief. I would like to introduce..., who will be your new GM (#2) for the Get Well Plan...We wish well to GM # 1, who has brought us to this stage, for his services. He has decided to leave to pursue other interests."

Reflection:

At the conclusion of "Bust the Bureaucracy" campaign, Mr. CEO replaced the managers of some other divisions as well. He had revealed in private to some people that he had taken care of the real sources of Bureaucracy. He felt that he had entrusted those fellows to run their business efficiently in first place, empowered them with all resources and compensated them very well. What had happened in the company should not have, if those people had not taken their eye off the ball from basics of running a business. He believed that they had violated his and the stockholders trust.

40.

When in Rome Do as the Romans Do

Humor in High Places:

From a speech of Ronald Reagan:

"On my first visit to Mexico, I gave a speech to a rather large audience and then sat down to rather unenthusiastic and scattered applause. I was embarrassed and tried to cover all of that, because what made it worse was that the next speaker up was speaking in Spanish, which I didn't understand, but he was getting interrupted virtually every line with most enthusiastic applause.

So, I started clapping before anyone else and longer than anyone else until our ambassador leaned over and said to me, 'I wouldn't do that if I were you. He is translating your speech.'"

Story Line:

If it can happen to Presidents, then who are we (common people) not to do such foolish things in a foreign land?

During one of my trips to Manila, I was invited to give an opening speech at a Quality & Reliability Conference. As I was sitting in the front seat waiting for my name to be called, I suddenly noticed that the entire audience had stood up.

Not knowing what was it for, maybe for me, I got up in a hurry. As I stood up, I noticed an elegant lady walking down the aisle. I assumed that she must be some famous celebrity guest of honor for the event.

Deciding to be proactive this time, I started clapping to welcome her.

Soon I noticed that I was the only one clapping, and many in the audience were trying to hold their laughter. I guess they had to. After all, I was the guest speaker. One colleague was frantically sending me some hand signals to stop clapping.

I immediately sat down, embarrassed again.

A few seconds later, I noticed (again!) that everyone was still standing and the lady had gone on to the podium and started a prayer. I found out later that it is customary in that part of the world to open the first event on the first Friday of the month with a prayer.

So, again, I got up in a hurry and prayed with others and ask for forgiveness for my foolish acts in a foreign land.

I guess my prayers were heard and at the end of my opening speech I got a long applause.

And mind you, I did not clap with the audience.

41.

If everyone deserves a "C" then every one will get one

In real life, grades do not produce value. The value is in how effectively the learning is applied.

Story Line:

In the summer of 1974, I took an Applied Mathematics class under Professor Ho. During the very first class, while Professor Ho was going over the course curriculum, some students repeatedly kept asking questions about his grading system. When asked one too many times, Professor Ho said, "Well, if everyone deserves a C then everyone will get one."

The next class was half the size of the first one. Many students had decided to drop out after listening to Professor Ho's explanation of his grading system.

At the end of the semester, when the day of reckoning arrived, we were astonished to see that everyone had gotten either an A or B. There were no grades lower.

My curiosity got the better of me and I asked Professor Ho, "If this is what the end result is, why did you scare off half the students with your comment about C grades in the first meeting?"

According to Professor Ho, the primary purpose of going to school should be learning, and not finding ways to manage or manipulate indicators like grades to get by. "Jumping from one class to another or from one Professor to another just to get grades does not build a strong foundation or lasting learning, which is neither a benefit to the students or to society."

Reflection:

Later, Professor Ho revealed a secret that some students had not done well in the exams (one time sitting) but he graded them based on his observation of how much commitment they had demonstrated in real learning and effort. He believed that those students would go a long way in life and career.

42.

When the feeling/passion is not there... the music is gone

Passion is the fuel that produces great performances

Story Line:

In the early 80s, during my assignment in Manila, one wise man told us the following story:

There was once a man who had accomplished many great things in his business. He was so successful in his ventures that business was growing in leaps and bounds. Money seemed to be falling off the tree.

In spite of his good fortune, every night he would come home tired and stressed, his mind still occupied with what was left through the day's work.

But as his luck would have it, in the late evening as he would lie down to bed trying hard to sleep, he would hear soothing sounds coming from a flute some distance away. Somehow that sound would melt all the stress and he would go into a sound sleep, and wake up fresh in the morning to encounter the next day's challenges.

Realizing the positive value of this music, he sent his men to find the source. Upon their return, his men reported that the source of that music was a man named Jimmy who lived in the squatter's camp outside the businessman's estate.

Jimmy was very poor and had to struggle to make a daily living for his family. But every night after dinner, Jimmy would sit down with his family and play his not so modern flute that produced such beautiful music. His family would enjoy the music, talk, giggle, and then retire for the day.

The businessman felt very sad that the person who provided such a great value to him was in a miserable financial state. So he offered Jimmy a job and a small residence on his estate. In exchange Jimmy would play music for him, and occasionally for his work functions.

Soon the businessman realized that in helping Jimmy, he could even help himself on a much larger scale if he could turn Jimmy's talents into a business; a business of concerts and training. Jimmy was given a better flute and a crew.

Jimmy became very popular and got called to perform in many places in many distant lands. There was not a time in the day for Jimmy to do anything but focus on this growing venture. His wife and children were lucky to even see Jimmy, and the evening music became a memory of the past.

After a few months, people started noticing that Jimmy's music was not what it used to be. Jimmy noticed it too.

So one day, Jimmy walked in to the businessman's office, and told him that he was returning to his old job.

Surprised, the businessman asked, "Have I not done enough to reward you for your work? Do you need a raise?"

Jimmy, while expressing his gratitude to the businessman, told him, "When I played flute before, I did it well because I loved doing it. It brought joy to my family and neighbors alike. I put my heart and soul into it."

Jimmy continued, "Now, I am too preoccupied with schedules, travels and other business issues; things that I neither understand well enough nor enjoy doing. I know money and position is good but the spark, the passion, that I had for what I did is no longer the driving factor. I don't even have time for my family or you as well Sir, who enjoyed my nightly music."

Jimmy had made a choice about what he wanted out of his life and the consequences that came with that choice.

Reflection:

As the wise man from Manila finished telling us the story he said, "Remember this story while nurturing talents in young children, developing people in any field as well as managing your own career. Keep in mind what brings one alive; what is one's passion. Pushing people beyond their core competency to do what they don't enjoy will only dry up that very music that produces great value."

43.

Cream or Sugar?

"Each friend represents a world in us, a world possibly not born until they arrive, and it is only by this meeting that a new world is born."

- Anaïs Nin

Story Line:

A few years ago, a fellow received a message from a well-wisher: "Congratulations on a well deserved promotion. The cream always rises to the top. Best Wishes."

The newly promoted fellow replied, "Thanks for your confidence and well wishes. As far as being the cream, I'll rather be the sugar instead. It is easy to scrape off the cream but the sugar mixes with milk and makes it sweeter."

I guess the promoted fellow was sharing something from a story he had learned in his childhood.

In the 7th century, a fleet of ships consisting of people who had fled Persia due to the change of regime arrived at the western shores of India. They were looking for a place to migrate and make their new home.

Since they spoke a different language, the king of a small state in India sent his emissary with a glass full of milk to communicate to the visitors that he had no space in his kingdom for more people.

The head of the fleet poured a spoon full of sugar in the glass of milk and sent it back to the king of the Indian state.

The king was first amused at the returned glass of milk but then he tasted it. His face lit up realizing that the message from the visitors was, "We will mix with your people and integrate into your community just like sugar mixes in milk and makes it sweeter."

And how true were they to their word? Zoroastrians or Parsis as they are known in India, is a community of 100,000 in a country of 1 Billion people. Their contributions in industry, art, science and literature are disproportionately tremendous. Just to mention a few Parsis: Zubin Mehta world famous conductor, Tata family- founder of many industries and Air India, Homi Bhabha the founder of India's Nuclear Program, Dadabhoy Navroji- a co-founder of modern India in Gandhi's team, Godrej family- large industrialist, and so many more...

I guess it takes only a small amount of sugar (.01% of the population) to add a lot of sweetness to the large pot of milk.

Reflection:

When you go to a new environment: whether it is a country or a company or an organization, mix with the local culture and use your talents in such a way that it enhances the capabilities of your new organization.

44.

The Story of Phar Lap: Don't judge by first appearance...and don't give up on people too soon

"It is not the color of the skin but the content of the character that matters."

- Dr. Martin Luther King

Story Line:

History shows that every crisis brings about new opportunities and new heroes. They come at the right time, when the world needs them the most, and many also leave when their purpose is accomplished. Here is a story of one such hero.

He emerged at the beginning of The Great Depression (1929) when the unemployment rate in Australia had reached 30%. The people were emotionally drained and had lost all hope. He left in 1932, just when the depression was ending.

But what he did in-between those years, made all the difference and, 75 years after his premature death, he remains Australia's national legend. With his tremendous spirit and heart of a champion, he injected the badly needed tonic of hope in despaired and discouraged nation by demonstrating that a plain old nobody, an average Joe, with a strong perseverance and drive can rise to the top even under the most difficult circumstances.

Conventional wisdom would associate heroes with humans. In the words of his trainer Harry Telford, "He was an angel. A human being couldn't have more sense. He was almost human; could do anything but talk." But Phar Lap was a horse born in New Zealand.

His new owner in Australia thought that they had struck a bargain until they saw him when he arrived at Sydney Harbor. Phar Lap's face was covered with warts, he did not look well bred and did not show any sign of being a horse that could be a champion.

The owner, Davis, was furious. Davis wanted to write him off as a bad investment and get rid of it. But Harry Tedford, the trainer, had faith in his selection and agreed to bear all cost of training in exchange for keeping him.

The rest is what history is made of. Harry, along with his assistant Tom Woodcock, raised Phar Lap with patience and love. Phar Lap lost the first eight of the nine races. But between September 1929 and April 1932, the period of the great depression, Phar Lap came first in 36 of the 41 races. He won every big race on the continent. In many of those races he was way behind until the last lap and emerged a winner.

As the next challenge, he was brought to America to compete against the best there. Despite a long and strenuous sea journey and a severely injured hoof, Phar Lap won America's richest race, Agua Caliente, in a record time while carrying 130 pounds.

As fate would have it, a few days later, he died in Menlo Park, California (Silicon Valley of today) of severe stomach ailments. He left the entire Australian continent mourning.

Phar Lap had defied many odds, including attempts on his life, and brought hope and emotional uplift to a continent devastated by severe depression. He was the hero the people most needed, a common guy with humble beginnings but with the heart of a champion, who never gave up and triumphed during the greatest economic tragedy.

Reflection:

Credit goes to the manager Harry Telford and the coach Tom Woodcock for believing in Phar Lap, being patient with him in the initial stages, and helping the newcomer to realize his full potential instead of immediately writing him off as a bad investment as the owner intended to do.

45.

Lessons about life from Vajubhai, our school principal

No human being is inferior to another just because of his birth or because of his work.

Story Line:

Teachers are the backbone of a nation. Next to parents, they are most instrumental in instilling good values in children. Those values shape not only the children's future but that of a society as a whole.

Our principal in school, Vajubhai, was one such great teacher. He believed that education was more important than just literacy. He introduced curriculums that were not just focused on classroom book learning but also on real life education.

One such "educational" event that happened annually was an Appreciation Day for all the educators. That was the day where students were to thank all the people who made it possible for their education, every individual involved in keeping the entire system operational.

On Appreciation Day, we would gather in an assembly hall or an open field. All those who made our education possible: teachers, administrative assistants, book keepers, bus drivers, yard cleaners and janitors were recognized and students would thank them.

There was one part of this event that was controversial. This is where our janitor, Trikam, would be invited on the stage and asked to raise the school flag. Then we would sing the school anthem and after that, salute Trikam. This was to be followed by a handshake with him. There was not a year when I did not notice tears in Trikam's eye during this part of the ceremony.

Now many would wonder, "What was so controversial about this?" Well, Trikam was not only a janitor but he was from the lower class of society classified as an "Untouchable." To have upper class kids, most of them from wealthy families, salute a "lowly" worker and then shake hands with him was not something that was tolerated by some people in those days.

When this event was first introduced, it had created uproar. Some wealthy donors had cancelled their money contributions and also pulled their children out of the school. Additionally, every year some parents were displeased that their children were being asked to participate. Some had even asked or warned to keep their children away from the "Hand Shake" part of the ceremony.

However, Vajubhai did not give in, and in the process he taught some very important lessons about life that many years after, some of us still fondly remember and talk about during reunions.

Reflection:

The lessons (education) that Vajubhai instilled in students were:

1. Every human being must be treated with respect and recognized for his or her contributions.
2. He did not compromise on his believes and values even when pressured with cancellation of crucial donations.

46.

Diversity and Communication

"The greatest problem of communication is the illusion that it has been accomplished."

—George Bernard Shaw

Story Line:

This increasingly connected world offers us great opportunities to learn about many countries and cultures. It also creates some unique challenges in communication and offers opportunities to participate in or witness some real humorous episodes. What the British mean by the words "hood" and "boot" is different than how the Americans interpret it. The Americans would be totally lost with words "capsicum" (bell pepper) and "brinjal" (eggplant) and most of the Indians may wonder what is, "the pepper with bell" or "the plant that makes eggs?" How about telling most of our first generation immigrant or foreign employees before the presentation, "break a leg"?

Here are few of many real stories that I have experienced through the years of working with other cultures and countries:

1. Bottom Line: In 1985, I was working for a small start up company. We were going to announce our flagship product. Our CEO wanted to take pictures of some sample units for an advertisement.

A SOS call was made to our overseas subcontractor for quick delivery. I gave marking instructions for the samples to the overseas fellow (Mr. Subcon) as follows:

Top Line:	Company Name
Second Line:	Product Code
3rd Line:	Manufacturing Lot number
Final line:	(c) 1984.

Mr. Subcon asked me if I had a preference for the type of ink for the marking. I said, "Mr. Subcon, I will leave that up to you. THE BOTTOM LINE *(key point)* is that the sample units have to look good."

After a few minutes of absolute silence, Mr. Subcon told me, "I am afraid that this is not possible. Your new bottom line has 28 characters. We can only put maximum of 14 characters in one line."

I was very thankful to Mr. Subcon for clarifying. I can't imagine what would have happened if the samples came with the marking, "The sample units have to look good."

2. "Song and Dance Story:" During one of my overseas assignments, a colleague and I were approached by a puzzled local quality manager. He had just received a message from an American sales manager that a customer would be visiting our overseas facility. He wanted the local quality manager to give a regular "Song and Dance Story" *(standard presentation)* to the customer. Our overseas quality manager explained to us that in their culture, "Song and Dance" could not be

performed in the company conference rooms. He could arrange that only in the Karaoke Bar.

3. "Maverick" lot initiative: Companies often use labeled initiatives like Six Sigma, TQM to reenergize masses and reinvent themselves. So in the early 90s, when one big corporation came out with a "maverick" lot initiative, my mid-size company decided to communicate the new requirements to the entire supply base.

Now the intent behind this label was to eliminate freak populations; once in awhile nonconforming material lots amongst mostly good lots.

While the keynote speech was in full swing, my colleague and I noticed that some of our overseas suppliers looked very confused. They had opened dictionaries and were making notes. We went for the rescue and noticed that they had copied the meanings of "maverick" from the dictionary as:

a. An orphaned calf (baby cow)
b. A horse that has escaped from the herd (team)
c. An independently minded person who refuses to abide by the rules of a particular group.

It took a while for us to explain the context of "maverick" in the new initiative and reassure our confused visitors that the company had no intention to diversify to cattle business. We were still in the semiconductor business and they had come to the right conference.

4.   A visitor at a hotel reception desk in a foreign land: "Is there an Italian restaurant close by?
Receptionist: "Close by 9PM."

Reflection:

While interacting in this diverse and global world, be careful in using slang. Also, close the communication loop by confirming that the intended message has been received by the other party.

47.

How to avoid the fate of the Boiled Frog

"Even if you are on the right track you will get run over if you just sit there."

—*Will Rogers*

Story Line:

The following parable has been used in many management and self development seminars to emphasis importance of being alert about the environmental changes and constantly updating skills to keep with the times.

If a frog is put in a pot full of boiling water, it will immediately jump out of it. But if you put him in a pot of cold water, he will stay there. Then if you start heating that pot, the frog will start enjoying the warmth of the water and may even start taking leisurely swim around the pot. Eventually the water gets hot enough where the Frog's internal system is paralyzed and the frog boils.

In the first scenario, a sudden change in the environment immediately alerted the frog's internal survival system. It reacted by jumping out. In the second scenario, the frog failed to notice gradual changes and negative trends that were threat to his existence.

So often, people fall into this trap. Like the frog they get complacent: "Benefits are good (water is getting lukewarm), the company is doing well (wow! the water is getting warmer and comfortable; let me take another lap), my bonus targets are good (let me take more leisurely laps), and I will retire here and live happily there after (internal system is almost paralyzed but I don't notice it)."

While enjoying such perks, they fail to see that the competition is getting intense; both in the business environment with other companies and in personal environment with a large pool of new comers entering the employment scene. And just like the poor frog, they get boiled without even noticing it.

Reflection:

Keep an eye on gradual changes in your environment, keep on learning new skills and assume responsibility. That will help you in avoiding the fate of the frog.

48.

The story of a good man

"We have flown the air like birds and swum the sea like fishes, but have yet to learn the simple act of walking the earth like brothers."

- Martin Luther King, Jr.

Story Line:

There is an old story of a man who lived as well as he could but along the way, he did commit a few sins.

When he died, his sins required him to spend a short time in hell before going up to heaven.

Hell didn't look that bad to him. There were no fires and the food was plentiful, looked and smelled delicious. But everyone seemed aggravated.

You see, in hell, the spoons were longer than people's arms. Every time they tried to place the spoon full of food in their mouths, food would drop over their shoulders. They were cranky because though they were so hungry, and could smell the delicious food, they could not get the food in their mouth.

Finally, the man was transferred to heaven.

Upon entering heaven, he smelled the same delicious food and could not wait to curb his hunger. Heaven looked exactly the same as hell. Everything was pleasant and he saw the same spoons in heaven as he had in hell. Shocked for a moment, he noticed everyone in heaven was happy. With the same food and long spoons, he wondered why.

You see, in spite of the large spoons, the people in heaven were able to enjoy the delicious food because they helped each other out and fed each other.

Reflection:

"Teamwork is the ability to work together toward a common vision, the ability to direct individual accomplishments toward organizational objectives. It is the fuel that allows common people to attain uncommon results."

—Andrew Carnegie

49.

"An ounce of loyalty is better than a pound of cleverness"—Elbert Hubbard

"Somebody once said that in looking for people to hire, you look for three qualities: integrity, intelligence, and energy. And if they don't have the first, the other two will kill you. You think about it; it's true. If you hire somebody without the first, you really want them to be dumb and lazy."

- Warren Buffett

Story Line:

Temujin, or Genghis Khan as we know him, was a great thirteenth century Mongol warrior who had conquered more land in 25 years than the Romans did in 400 years. In the process he connected many civilizations from Europe to Asia. He abolished the old system based on special privilege for the rich and introduced a more equitable system based on qualifications and accomplishments. He lived the simple life of a nomad, distributed his wealth to people and established a fair system based on law and order.

In war he was ruthless but in friendship he was kind. He valued loyalty as a very important trait in people.

In the early 13th century, the Mongol forces finally defeated their archrival Jamuka once and for all. Jamuka fled to distant mountains with some of his soldiers. The life in exile was very difficult and hard to handle for soldiers who had prospered under Jamuka and were used to life of affluence. Unable to cope with the harsh life, they tied up their leader and took him to Temujin hoping for amnesty and a handsome reward.

Guess what Temujin did to those soldiers?

Temujin executed them all.

But to his opponent he was gracious, and asked Jamuka to join him.

Reflection:

For Temujin, loyalty was not selective for good times and richness only.

What do you think those soldiers would have done to him if he was having tough times?

It is in the bad times that a persons' loyalty is truly tested.

50.

First Stage in the acceptance of a new idea

All truth passes through three stages: First, it is ridiculed; Second, it is violently opposed; and Third, it is accepted as self-evident.

—Arthur Schopenhauer, 1788-1860

First, you know, a new theory (idea) is attacked as absurd; then it is admitted to be true, but obvious and insignificant; finally it is seen to be so important that its adversaries claim that they themselves discovered it.

- William James 1907

Story Line:

So many ideas have been rejected when first proposed.

Barry Marshall and Robin Warren were ridiculed by the establishment and booed off the stage at scientific meetings for their idea that most ulcers were caused by certain bacteria and not stress as popularly believed. They won the 2005 Nobel Prize for their discovery.

Fred Smith's paper about an overnight delivery service got a "C" grade at Yale for not being a feasible idea. He later founded Federal Express using the same idea.

Alexander Graham Bell's offer to sell his patent on the telephone was rejected by the president of Western Union. He called the telephone, "nothing but a toy." Internal experts at Western Union had concluded that the telephone had too many shortcomings to be considered as a means of communication.

David Sarnoff's business plan seeking venture funding for the Radio was rejected with a comment, "The wireless music box has no imaginable commercial value. Who would pay for a message sent to nobody in particular?"

Louis Pasteur's theory of germs was termed "ridiculous fiction," by a well-known professor.

This is what Ken Olson, founder of a Digital Equipment, said about the idea of a Personal Computer, "There is no reason for any individual to have a computer in his home." His other famous words were: "UNIX is snake oil."

And to top all of the above, the words of Charles H. Duell, Commissioner, U.S. Office of Patents, 1899, "Everything that can be invented has been invented."

Reflection:

Instead of getting demoralized and giving up, the inventors believed in themselves and the strength of their ideas. They stayed on course and realized the fulfillment of their vision.

So what are your ideas that have been rejected?

1................................
2................................

51.

What is your excuse?

"Our only real handicaps are those mental and emotional ones that prevent us from participating fully in life"

-John Foppe

Storyline:

What is your excuse? Making the most of what you have (Life story of John Foppe)

In mid 90s, I was invited to attend a seminar on leadership. Before I went, I was wondering, "What would I learn about leadership from this 24 year old guest speaker named John Foppe?" But having read that he had spoken in front of the Pentagon people, many chief executives of large corporations, and sports teams around the world, I decided to take a chance with my time.

The master of ceremonies stated that John had a master's degree in clinical social work with top honors and that he also drove a car himself. As the seminar progressed, this young man displayed how to open a can of coke, pour coke into a glass and then drink it. He also demonstrated his writing ability, his ability to wear clothes and put a tie on. He was a great speaker, displayed a tremendous sense of humor and inspired the audience with many lessons from his life.

Now you may wonder "What is so unique about all these accomplishments?"

Well, John was born without both arms. But he had decided very early in life that he was going to make the best use of whatever resources he had, instead of dwelling on what others would have considered a handicap. He had learnt to do many things with his feet. John Foppe taught us that "our only real handicaps are those mental and emotional ones that prevent us from participating fully in life."

Reflection:

In these times of "resource constraints", it is worth reading some of John's work and to learn his creative problem solving skills. They offer a totally new perspective about life and making the best use of what we have.

52.

Lessons in Leadership from the life of Walter Payton

Lives of great men all remind us we can make our lives sublime, and departing, leave behind us footprints on the sands of time.

-Longfellow, A Psalm of Life

You cannot expect to do well in one compartment of life while not doing well in the other. Life is one indivisible whole.

- Mahatma Gandhi

Story Line:

Walter Payton, a man called sweetness and the star of Chicago Bear's Super Bowl Victory was voted as one of the top ten football players of all time.

Walter's job description at the time of recruitment was that of a running back. Weighing less than 200lbs., he would go against a wall of 300+lbs. defensive linesmen; and tackle them with so much force that they would fall and Walter would get through. If he did not find the hole, he would turn around and go sideways to find another way to get ahead.

Whenever he was not the primary ball carrier, he would block for his colleagues. At times, he would throw or punt the ball as well. Walter did not consider himself as just a running back but a football player who gave everything he had for one purpose, a chance for his team to win.

After the game, he would wait to sign autographs for every kid who was waiting. (No child left behind).

In the super bowl, the coach asked William "The Refrigerator" Perry to carry the ball from one yard for the touchdown instead of Walter, as most would have expected. Walter felt hurt but never criticized the coach.

In his last two seasons, recognizing that his time in football was limited, he showed true professionalism and became the mentor to younger teammates looking to fill his role.

He is a hero to many people, a role model of what a great human being should be, not only because of his unique style of running and the records he piled up, but because what he did off the field as well.

On the field he gave everything he had for his team to win; and off the field he devoted his life to family, friends and charities for underprivileged children. His teammates and fans alike loved him and named him "a man called sweetness."

In 1999, when faced with a rare liver disease, Walter was offered an option to move up in the waiting list for an organ donation because of his popularity and celebrity. He refused, stating that he did not want to deny someone else an opportunity to live just because of his status. Recognizing that there are millions of people who were in need of an organ, he went on national TV and inspired people to become organ donors. He did all these while knowing that he could not get one for himself in time because of many others on the waiting list before him.

Walter Payton was not just a leader in football; he was true leader in life and in death.

Walter's Last Message to the World

From <u>Never Die Easy, The autobiography of Walter Payton</u> by Don Yaeger,

"If you ask me how I want to be remembered, it is as a winner. You know what a winner is? A winner is somebody who has given his best effort, who has tried the hardest they possibly can, who has utilized every ounce of energy and strength within them to accomplish something. It does not mean they accomplished it or failed, it means they have given it their best. That is a winner."

"All those honors are great, but personally I would ask that anyone who wants to pay tribute to me, for any reason, I would say there is one thing you could do above everything else and that is: Never let a day go by where you neglect to tell your loved ones that you love them. For you never know what tomorrow may have in store. Remember, tomorrow is promised to no one."

Reflection:

I would like to end the first year of *Friday Reflections* with a tribute to Walter, my hero and a hero to millions of people, with two beautiful quotes:

"To live in the hearts we leave behind is not to die."
                                                    -Thomas Campbell

"What we once enjoyed, we can never lose. All that we love deeply becomes a part of us."
                                                    -Helen Keller

Reflecting on Reflections

In ancient times, storytelling was one of the major means of education. Elders would pass on their experiences, their triumphs and tragedies, to the next generation by telling tales. In many cultures, the time after evening meals was allocated for stories. The experiences were communicated mostly through fables and real life events. Each story had some moral to instill good values.

In modern busy times, this practice, though not as widely spread as before, still continues in many cultures and families.

Each Friday, on evening rides with our children, I would tell stories from events that happened in the office or in the world; from the books I read, or from the stories from my own childhood, which were told by great teachers or by my own parents during evening rides with them. In some stories, the names of the people are changed out of respect for them and also to protect their privacy.

The proof of pudding is in eating and the value of book is in reading. I hope you found as much value in these stories as the friends who have received *Friday Reflections* over the last several years.

Anand P. Shah

Preview of Friday Reflection Volume 2: Web of Life.

"All things are connected. Whatever befalls the earth befalls the sons and daughters of the earth. Man did not weave the web of life; he is merely a strand in it. Whatever he does to the web, he does to himself."

There is much controversy about who said the beautiful words of the above quote: Chief Seattle in 1854 or Ted Perry in 1970. Instead of dwelling in the controversy of who said those words; most important thing is to focus on what is being said in those words. They represent the wisdom of the ages from every culture and follow the Golden Rule.

The theme for *Friday Reflections Volume 2: The Web of Life*, revolves around the concept that many things in nature are part of a massive dynamic system. There are strong interrelationships and interdependencies in our environment. And in this context, the word "environment" has a very wide scope: nature, earth, job, business, relationships, home etc.

In a dynamic system, actions and the reactions to actions are often separated in time and space. What we do today could have tremendous, positive or negative, consequences in the future.

Through many real life stories and examples, the book coveys the key message about the importance of maintaining a healthy eco-system; whether it is related to personal things, professional things or to our encounters with nature. Even in a dynamic system that we live in, one thing has not changed through the ages: "As we sow, so shall we reap."

Upcoming Products

When published, these upcoming products will be available at http://analisaenterprises.com:

- Friday Reflection Volume 2: The Web of Life
- Xena Doolittle
- East West Personality Profiles
- Significance of being insignificant
- My life as a baseball
- All that glitters is not gold
- My Lola

Friday Reflections on the Web

Visit us on the Internet at http://fridayreflections.com

- See the newest & latest weekly reflections
- Share your own reflections with the world
- Preview our exciting upcoming products in the area of education and entertainment
- Purchase Friday Reflections in many formats, including affordable and convenient eBooks

Author Biography

Originally from India, Anand Shah earned his Masters in Engineering Administration from Stanford University and his Masters in Electrical Engineering from the University of Southern California. An executive and consultant for successful start-ups and major corporations in Silicon Valley for over thirty years, his previous book Other Mothers have Problems, Too was published in 1988. Married to his childhood pen pal, he and his wife have two children and reside in the San Francisco Bay area.